ZODIAC SIGNS

TAURUS

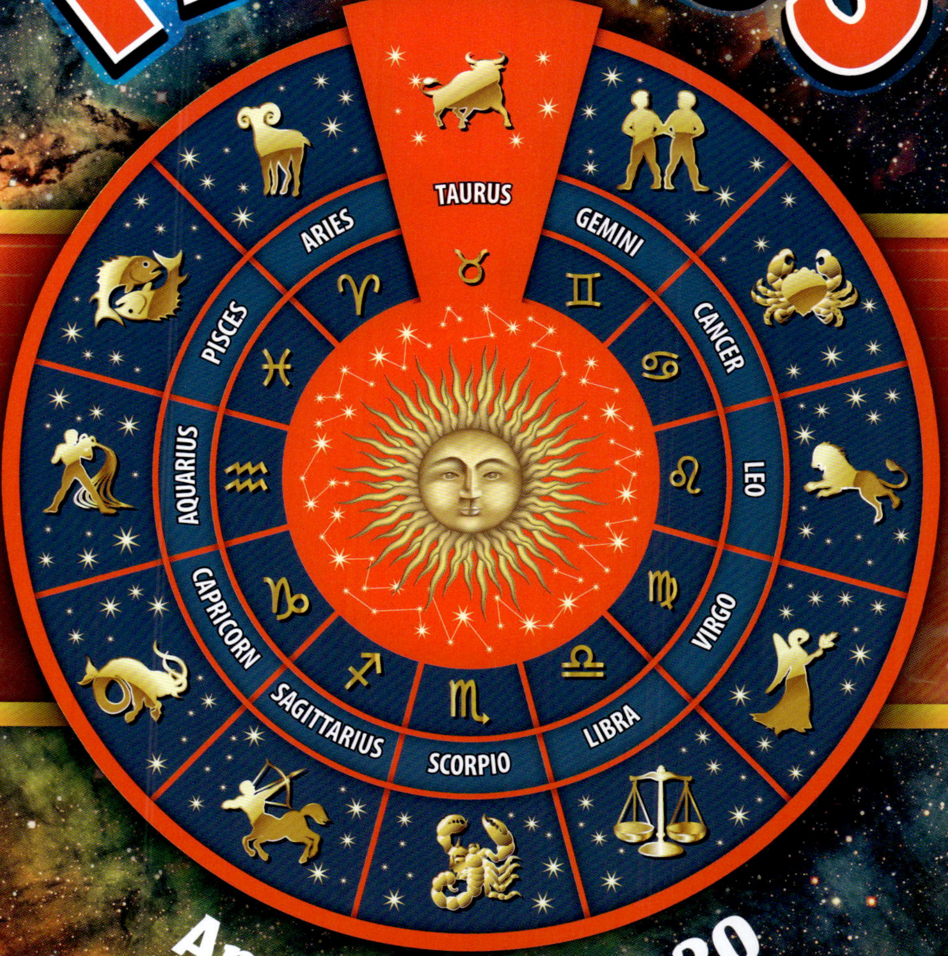

April 20 – May 20

Katie Gillespie

AV2
www.av2books.com

Step 1
Go to **www.av2books.com**

Step 2
Enter this unique code
WQYPXNQSC

Step 3
Explore your interactive eBook!

AV2 is optimized for use on any device

Your interactive eBook comes with...

Contents
Browse a live contents page to easily navigate through resources

Audio
Listen to sections of the book read aloud

Videos
Watch informative video clips

Weblinks
Gain additional information for research

Try This!
Complete activities and hands-on experiments

Key Words
Study vocabulary, and complete a matching word activity

Quizzes
Test your knowledge

Slideshows
View images and captions

... and much, much more!

TAURUS

April 20 – May 20

Contents

Are You a Taurus?

Do people call you trustworthy? Are you considered to be reliable? If this sounds familiar, you might be a Taurus. A Taurus is someone who was born between April 20 and May 20.

Taurus is a sign in the zodiac. This is a series of 12 **constellations** that run across the night sky. For centuries, people have used these groups of stars to tell the future. The study of the stars in this manner is called astrology.

Zodiac Chart

A person's zodiac sign is determined by his or her date of birth. Which sign matches your birthday?

It's in the Stars

The zodiac constellations form a circle around Earth. In one year, Earth makes a full **orbit** around the Sun. As it does this, the Sun appears to be in different places at set times. The zodiac constellations are found along the path the Sun follows.

Long ago, people used the Sun to tell the time of year. In late April, the Sun passed through the Taurus constellation. People born then were said to be born under the sign of Taurus.

Over time, the position of the constellations shifted. Even though the Sun now passes through Taurus at a different time, the dates associated with the sign of Taurus remain the same.

Taurus is famous for its **Pleiades**, or **Seven Sisters** star cluster. Its stars represent the **daughters** of the Greek god **Atlas**.

Aldebaran is the brightest star in **Taurus** and the **14th brightest star** in the **night sky**.

Taurus is one of the oldest known constellations. It is also called the Bull. Descriptions of it have been found as far back as the Bronze Age, more than 5,000 years ago.

The Myth of Taurus

The ancient Greeks had stories about how each zodiac constellation came to be in the sky. Taurus is linked to Zeus, the ruler of the Greek gods. Zeus could control rain, wind, thunder, and lightning.

Zeus was well known for his love affairs. On one such occasion, Zeus wanted to win the affections of Europa, the daughter of a **Phoenician** king. Transforming into a handsome white bull, Zeus joined the king's herd.

Europa came over to the new bull and sat on his back. Zeus quickly leaped into the sea and carried her to the island of Crete. There, he revealed his true self and gave Europa many gifts. The couple went on to have three sons.

Later, Zeus placed an image of the bull among the stars. This became the Taurus constellation.

As the continent of Europe was named after Europa, several European countries feature prominent sculptures of her. One of the best known is in London, England.

Taurus and Fixed Signs

In astrology, some zodiac signs share certain **qualities**. These qualities show how a person acts in the world. The qualities are separated into three groups. Cardinal signs are likely to get projects moving. Fixed signs help to calm situations. Mutable signs are able to go with the flow.

Taurus is a fixed sign. People in this group are known for being determined. They work hard to achieve their goals. Fixed signs are also persistent. They are able to stay focused even when obstacles get in their way.

Fixed signs such as Taurus have the discipline needed to take their ideas and make them a reality.

Zodiac Signs
by Quality

Cardinal Signs
Get projects moving.

Aries Cancer Libra Capricorn

Fixed Signs
Help to calm situations.

Taurus Leo Scorpio Aquarius

Mutable Signs
Go with the flow.

Gemini Virgo Sagittarius Pisces

Taurus as an Earth Sign

Zodiac signs are also grouped according to the four **classical elements**. These are fire, earth, water, and air. Signs that belong to the same group share common personality **traits**.

Taurus is an earth sign. Earth people are reasonable. They are good at making plans and putting them into action. Earth people are considered to be practical and hardworking. They can also be **ambitious**.

Earth people understand that goals are not always reached quickly. They are willing to work over the long term to achieve what they want from life.

Zodiac Signs
by Element

Being a Taurus

A Taurus's earth traits and fixed qualities combine to create a specific type of person. A key Taurus strength is loyalty. Taureans are always there for the people in their lives. They are romantic and deeply devoted.

Taureans have their weaknesses as well. They are sometimes viewed as stubborn. However, what may seem like stubbornness to some people can also be viewed as commitment or persistence by others.

The **zodiac** is divided into **12 houses**. Taurus is the ruler of the **2nd house**, the **house** of **money** and **possessions**.

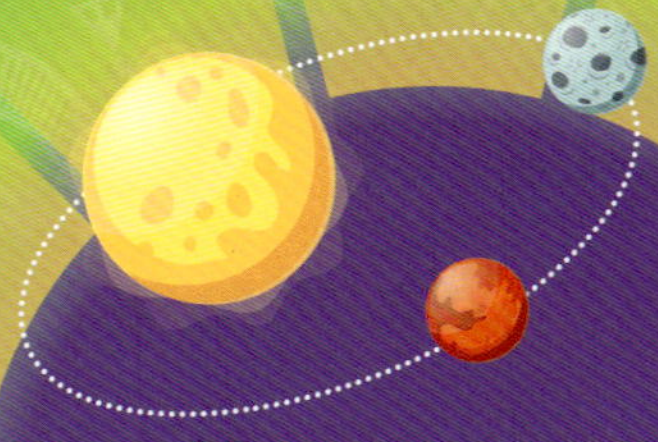

Venus is Taurus's **ruling planet**. Venus is the **2nd planet** from the **Sun** and the **closest** planet to **Earth**.

Taureans enjoy spending time with friends and can turn an ordinary day into a fun experience for all.

Taureans through Time

Taureans have had a significant impact on the world over time. They have written great works, painted **masterpieces**, and become important political leaders. Their contributions have helped make the world what it is today.

1603

The first known edition of *Hamlet*, by English playwright **William Shakespeare** (born around April 23, 1564), is published. *Hamlet* is often considered to be the best play of all time.

1838

Inventor **Samuel Morse** (born April 27, 1791) introduces Morse Code, a system of communication that uses dots and dashes in place of letters and numbers, for the first time.

1869

General **Ulysses S. Grant** (born April 27, 1822) becomes the 18th president of the United States.

1931

Spanish artist **Salvador Dali** (born May 11, 1904) paints *The Persistence of Memory*, now on display at the Museum of Modern Art in New York City.

2015

Queen Elizabeth II (born April 21, 1926) becomes the longest-ruling monarch in British history.

2020

Singer **Lizzo** (born April 27, 1988) wins three Grammy Awards out of eight nominations. These annual awards recognize achievements in the music industry.

Making Friends

Zodiac signs may affect the way people get along with others. Each sign has its own set of traits. Knowing which traits go well together could help people understand their relationships. A Taurus might be drawn to certain people based on their signs.

It's Friendship

Taureans get along well with people born under these signs.

Taurus

Pisces

Scorpio

It's Love

Taureans often find romance with these signs.

Cancer

Virgo

Capricorn

It's Complicated

Taureans find it difficult to form bonds with these signs.

Leo

Aquarius

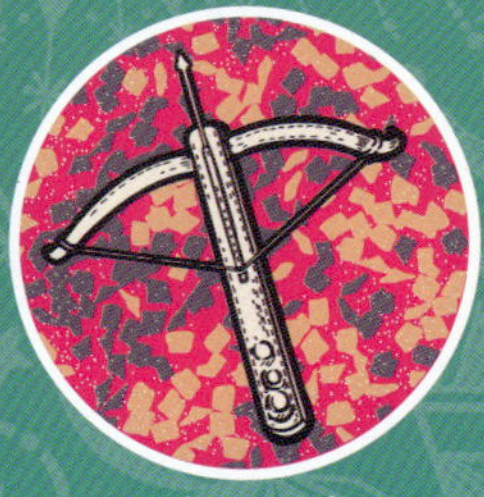

Sagittarius

Know Your Taureans

Taureans continue to make an impact on the world. They can be found doing good work in various fields. Did you know these people are Taureans?

Dwayne "The Rock" Johnson

Born: May 2, 1972

Dwayne Johnson first rose to fame as a **professional** wrestler. As "The Rock," he was one of wrestling's biggest stars. After appearing in one of the popular *Mummy* films, Johnson decided to pursue acting full time. He has since starred in several hit movies, including the Disney film *Moana* and the *Jumanji* series.

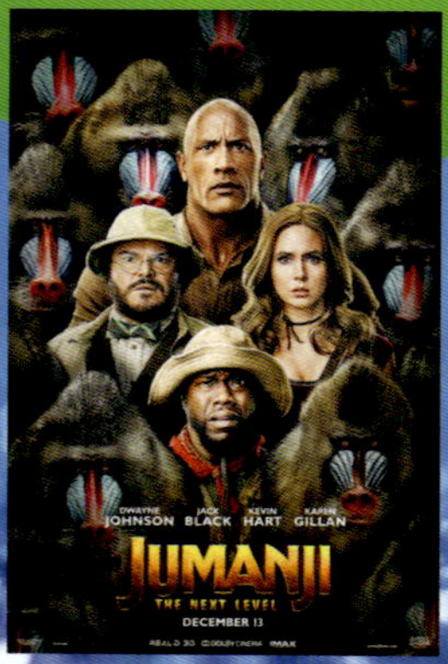

Jumanji: The Next Level was released in 2019. It earned almost $800 million worldwide.

Rob Gronkowski

Born: May 14, 1989

Rob Gronkowski was **drafted** into the National Football League (NFL) in 2010. During his nine seasons with the New England Patriots, he won three **Super Bowl** titles. Although he retired in 2019, Gronkowski plans to return to the game in 2020 as a member of the Tampa Bay Buccaneers.

JoJo Siwa

Born: May 19, 2003

JoJo Siwa first gained national attention on the television show *Dance Moms*. Since then, she has made a name for herself as a dancer, singer, and social media sensation, with more than 11 million subscribers on YouTube.

Gal Gadot

Born: April 30, 1985

Gal Gadot's path to stardom began with a win at the 2004 Miss Israel competition. After a successful career as a model, she made her film debut in the 2009 movie *Fast & Furious*. Gadot hit new levels of fame in 2016, when she was cast as Wonder Woman, a hugely popular superhero in the DC Universe.

Mark Zuckerberg

Born: May 14, 1984

Mark Zuckerberg is the co-founder of Facebook, the largest social networking website on the internet. Launched in 2004, Facebook now has more than 2.5 billion **active users** every month. This success has made Zuckerberg a billionaire. In 2020, he was ranked the seventh-richest person on the planet.

The Taurus QUIZ

1 What is the brightest star in Taurus?

2 With which zodiac signs do Taureans find it difficult to form bonds?

3 To which element group do Taureans belong?

4 How many Grammy Awards did Lizzo win in 2020?

5 Which Taurus was the 18th president of the United States?

6 Which Greek god is closely linked to the Taurus constellation?

7 In what year was Facebook founded?

8 Which planet rules Taurus?

ANSWERS: 1. Aldebaran 2. Leo, Aquarius, and Sagittarius 3. Earth 4. Three 5. Ulysses S. Grant 6. Zeus 7. 2004 8. Venus

Key Words

active users: people who visit or interact with an internet product

ambitious: having a strong desire to succeed

classical elements: materials from which all other materials were once believed to be made

constellations: groups of stars that form patterns in the sky

drafted: selected to play for a team

masterpieces: projects done with great skill

orbit: a regular, repeating path that one object in space takes around another

Phoenician: relating to an ancient civilization that existed in the area now known as Lebanon

professional: someone who is paid to do a job that people usually do as a hobby

qualities: traits that make something what it is

Super Bowl: the annual championship game of the National Football League

traits: distinguishing qualities or characteristics

Index

Get the best of both worlds.

AV2 bridges the gap between print and digital.

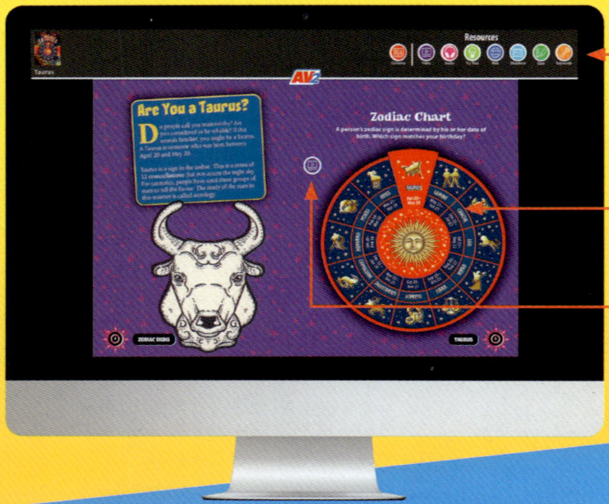

The expandable resources toolbar enables quick access to content including **videos**, **audio**, **activities**, **weblinks**, **slideshows**, **quizzes**, and **key words**.

Animated videos make static images come alive.

Resource icons on each page help readers to further **explore key concepts**.

Published by AV2
14 Penn Plaza 9th Floor
New York, NY 10122
Website: www.av2books.com

Library of Congress Control Number: 2020938562

ISBN 978-1-7911-2620-9 (hardcover)
ISBN 978-1-7911-2621-6 (softcover)
ISBN 978-1-7911-2622-3 (multi-user eBook)
ISBN 978-1-7911-2623-0 (single-user eBook)

Printed in Guangzhou, China
1 2 3 4 5 6 7 8 9 0 24 23 22 21 20

062020
101119

Editor: Heather Kissock
Designer: Terry Paulhus

Every reasonable effort has been made to trace ownership and to obtain permission to reprint copyright material. The publisher would be pleased to have any errors or omissions brought to their attention so that they may be corrected in subsequent printings.

AV2 acknowledges Getty Images, Alamy, Shutterstock, and iStock as its primary image suppliers for this title.